Workbook

PYP

Skills

Growth mindset
Self-motivation, Perseverance and Resilience

Dr Kimberley O'Brien

HODDER
EDUCATION
AN HACHETTE UK COMPANY

The Publishers would like to thank the following for permission to reproduce copyright material.

Photo credits: **p.8** © Monster Ztudio/stock.adobe.com; **p.16** © Brian Jackson/stock.adobe.com; **p.22** © Monkey Business/stock.adobe.com

Every effort has been made to trace all copyright holders, but if any have been inadvertently overlooked, the Publishers will be pleased to make the necessary arrangements at the first opportunity.

Although every effort has been made to ensure that website addresses are correct at time of going to press, Hodder Education cannot be held responsible for the content of any website mentioned in this book. It is sometimes possible to find a relocated web page by typing in the address of the home page for a website in the URL window of your browser.

Hachette UK's policy is to use papers that are natural, renewable and recyclable products and made from wood grown in well-managed forests and other controlled sources. The logging and manufacturing processes are expected to conform to the environmental regulations of the country of origin.

Orders: please contact Bookpoint Ltd, 130 Park Drive, Milton Park, Abingdon, Oxon OX14 4SE. Telephone: +44 (0)1235 827827. Fax: +44 (0)1235 400401. Email education@bookpoint.co.uk Lines are open from 9 a.m. to 5 p.m., Monday to Saturday, with a 24-hour message answering service. You can also order through our website: www.hoddereducation.com

© Dr Kimberley O'Brien 2020
First published in 2020 by
Hodder Education,
An Hachette UK Company
Carmelite House
50 Victoria Embankment
London EC4Y 0DZ
www.hoddereducation.com

Impression number   10 9 8 7 6 5 4 3 2 1

Year   2024 2023 2022 2021 2020

Illustrations by Hannah McCafferey

Typeset in VAG Rounded 14/20pt by DC Graphic Design Limited

Printed in Spain

A catalogue record for this title is available from the British Library.

ISBN: 9781510481619

Contents

Growth mindset

A `mindset` is the way we think about problems and challenges and the way we try to solve them. We often talk about two different mindsets: a `fixed mindset` or a `growth mindset`.

It can be disappointing when you don't do well at something. Sometimes, you might feel angry or frustrated with yourself for not getting it right. At these times, you can choose to have either a fixed mindset or a growth mindset.

A fixed mindset is associated with statements such as:	A growth mindset is associated with more worthwhile statements such as:
■ I can't.	■ I can learn this.
■ It's too hard.	■ I'll find a way.
■ I'll never get it.	■ I don't know this *yet*.

Having a growth mindset will help you to overcome challenges more easily. For example, when something difficult happens, you will be able to ask, 'It didn't go the way I hoped, but what can I learn from this?'

In this book, we will work together on ways in which you can build a growth mindset by increasing your self-motivation, perseverance and resilience.

- `Self-motivation` is thinking you can do something, and working towards it.

- `Perseverance` is about pushing ahead when progress is slow or difficult.

- `Resilience` is about teaching yourself to cope when things go wrong or are not as you expected.

Let's circle the words or phrases we often associate with a growth mindset.

improve   can't   plan B   try again

learn   no   train   practise

options   team   hard   feedback

flexible   open   difficult   new

growth   confusing   mindset   closed

mistakes   stupid   attempt

3

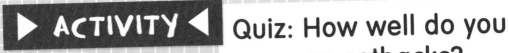

▶ ACTIVITY ◀ Quiz: How well do you manage setbacks?

Having a go is the most important part of learning. When you're brave enough to try something new, it's completely fine to get things wrong. The first step is to try. Don't worry about making mistakes. They're just minor ¡setbacks¡ and everything gets easier with practice!

Answer the questions below to see how well you cope with setbacks.

Question 1

Your teacher gives your class a page of maths problems to try but they look like nothing you've ever tried before! What do you do next?

A Start with the first question and do the best you can.

B Feel worried for a bit and then look for a question that might be a little easier to get started.

C Feel worried and unable to start: you don't know how to do these questions at all. What if you get them all wrong?

Question 2

A friend you met at art class invites you to her birthday party. When you arrive, you don't know anyone else there. What do you do?

A Take a deep breath and strike up a conversation with the first friendly-looking person you see.

B Look around the room until you spot your friend from art class. Then go over to her and stay with her for the whole party.

C Make a run for it! Your mum might still be outside.

Question 3

Have you ever tried something and failed? Is it true that practice makes perfect?

A Yes! You can get better at anything if you try for long enough.

B Maybe. Some things are harder than others, so it's not always true.

C No! You are either good at something or you're not.

Question 4

You thought you did really well in a spelling test but you actually failed. What do you do next?

A Speak to your teacher, or a parent or carer, about what went wrong and how you can do better next time.

B Feel frustrated but decide to try harder on the next test.

C Decide that spelling is something you're just not good at and focus your efforts on maths instead.

Question 5

Your teacher gives you some feedback about a project you did and suggests how you could improve. How does this make you feel?

A Grateful – tips from your teacher are always helpful!

B Embarrassed – it's hard to hear that you could do better.

C Angry – you did your best and feedback is a waste of time.

Grade your quiz

Give yourself 3 points for every C answer you chose, 2 points for every B answer and 1 point for every A answer. Add up your points.

Your score: _____/15

Now look at the table below to find out about your mindset.

5 points	Well done! You have a growth mindset. With this mindset, you can face setbacks with confidence and work on improvement.
6–10 points	Your mindset is quite mixed at the moment. There are times when you believe you can face setbacks and improve, but in other situations, you give up more easily. You've made a good start though, so well done!
11–15 points	Your mindset is quite fixed at the moment, but don't worry – the great thing about building a growth mindset is that everyone can do it!

▶ REFLECTION ◀

Were you surprised by your quiz results?

How do you feel about building your growth mindset?

1 Self-motivation

Motivation is the feeling or impulse that encourages you to do certain things, such as getting a glass of water when you are thirsty. Being thirsty *motivates* you to get a drink.

Sometimes, you will be motivated by others – for example, if you are told you can watch TV as long as you tidy your room first. At other times, you will be self-motivated – you do something because you want to. This might be to benefit yourself or another person, but it is your idea to make it happen.

You may feel motivated if you are offered a reward or you receive encouragement from others. You might also be motivated by music, or by human needs (such as feeling hungry).

Let's find out how to spark your motivation!

▶ ACTIVITY ◀ Self-motivation

Let's learn more about self-motivation.

Leo wanted to improve his basketball skills, so every day after school he practised shooting hoops. No one else asked him to do this: he did it because he was self-motivated.

How about you? Can you remember a time when you were self-motivated? Maybe you wanted to achieve a new goal or learn a new skill. Write about the experience here.

_____

_____

_____

_____

_____

_____

Have you ever stopped to consider what motivates you to do the things you like? How about the things you do not like? Let's explore your motivation profile.

Review the following situations. For each one, think about what would motivate you to do it and draw an arrow to show how much effort it would take. The first one has been done for you.

Situation	What would motivate you to do this?	Effort required
Swim at the beach	Feeling hot, feeling a bit restless, joining friends or family who are already swimming	Low / Normal / High
Eat a chocolate cake		Low / Normal / High
Practise your favourite sport		Low / Normal / High
Have a warm bath		Low / Normal / High

Situation	What would motivate you to do this?	Effort required
Study for a test or exam		Low Normal High
Have an injection		Low Normal High
Jump on soft snow		Low Normal High
Jump in an ice bath in winter		Low Normal High

Can you describe two strategies you use to motivate yourself?

1 _____
_____
_____

2 _____
_____
_____

Being self-motivated can be challenging! We know what we *should* do to achieve our goal, but actually *doing* it may be a different story. Let's consider some of the strategies we can use to spark our motivation, with the help of Akari and her dad, Kobe.

Step 1

Setting a goal

A clear goal can help us to feel motivated because it defines our next achievable step. Let's help Akari to set a goal.

Step 2

Making a plan or schedule

Often, you can make a clear step-by-step plan to help you feel motivated. You can record tasks, times and deadlines in a chart to keep track of your goals and achievements.

Step 3

Rewards

You can give yourself a small reward each time you reach a milestone or goal. This will encourage you to keep going.

Step 4

Positive self-talk/positive reinforcement

You can say motivating and positive things to yourself, such as 'Well done' or 'Keep going'. You can also ask other people to cheer you on or encourage you.

What strategy can you suggest to help Akari improve her spelling?

Strategy

_____

_____

_____

_____

Think about these situations. For each one, suggest a strategy to help Akari to self-motivate.

Situation

Akari really wants to improve her spelling, but every time she sits down to do her spelling practice, she seems to find something else to do.

Strategy

Akari gave herself one point for every word she tried to spell. 10 points = 10 minutes of extra reading time before bed.

13

Situation

Akari needs to clean her bedroom but she does not really want to. What might help?

Strategy

_____

_____

_____

_____

Situation

It is time for breakfast. Akari loves fresh fruit, but only if her dad cuts it. What can she do to get started?

Strategy

_____

_____

_____

_____

Situation

Akari is running late for school. How can she help herself to be more punctual?

Strategy

_____
_____
_____
_____

Can you think of any other ideas to help Akari be self-motivated?

_____
_____
_____
_____
_____
_____
_____
_____
_____
_____
_____
_____
_____
_____

2 What is positive thinking?

Positive thinking is when you use your thoughts to make you feel better. When you use positive words, like 'I can do this!', you start to feel self-motivated! This is also known as positive self-talk or positive reinforcement.

'I can't do that!' sounds negative because it suggests you are not willing to even try. When you think about something in a negative way, this can change the way you feel about it. This is known as negative self-talk.

Think about something like a school camp. Some people might say, 'I love camp!' while others say, 'Camp is the worst!' If you believe it is 'the worst', you probably won't want to go. You might even tell your parents, 'Camp is the worst'.

Thinking about something in a positive way can help you to feel like giving it a go!

Look at the pictures below. Colour in the characters who are showing a positive mindset.

▶ ACTIVITY ◀ Detective thinking

People often focus on what is not working and exaggerate the negative consequences of mistakes. However, with practice you can spot and change these behaviours.

Let's use our detective thinking to notice negative thoughts and replace them with more positive ones.

Step 1

Read the situations below. In each one, highlight a negative word or phrase.

1 I have never eaten this kind of food before. This is going to be horrible!

2 I cannot believe we are going to research this project by ourselves. It is going to be a disaster!

3 When I see a challenge, I run away from it.

4 I find spelling so difficult. I have never scored a good mark ever.

5 I do really well in some things, but in other things I'm a failure.

6 If you are not good at something, practice probably won't help you to improve.

7 When I am told I could do better, I feel angry.

8 I find it impossible to learn from my mistakes.

9 Some people are experts at things, but other people are not.

10 I have a fixed mindset, so I find setbacks frustrating.

Step 2

Turn to page 51. This page contains 11 positive words and phrases.

Cut them out and stick them over the negative words and phrases you identified in Step 1.

Then read the sentences again.

Step 3

Choose three of the sentences to discuss as a group. Think about these questions.

1   How did the negative sentences and words make you feel?

2   Did the positive words and sentences make you feel better?

3   How much effort did it take to make a negative idea more positive?

Write your thoughts here.

_____

_____

_____

_____

_____

_____

_____

_____

_____

_____

_____

_____

_____

Meet Negative Noel and Positive Pattie.

Noel has a very fixed mindset. He often finds it difficult to see a way forward. He tends to say negative things when he is faced with a challenge.

Noel's friend Pattie, however, tends to see things in a positive way. She shows a growth mindset.

In pairs, try the following role plays.

Instructions

Choose one person to be Noel and one person to be Pattie.

If you are Pattie, your role is to help Noel to use a growth mindset instead of a fixed mindset.

Take turns, so you both have a chance to play Pattie.

Role-play scenarios

1 Noel is waiting for his turn at the handball court. He says out loud, 'I always get out on my first turn.'

How can Pattie help Noel to change his fixed mindset to a growth mindset?

2 In the classroom, the teacher has just explained the next activity. Noel drops his pencil and says, 'That's too hard for me to do.'

How can Pattie help Noel to change his fixed mindset to a growth mindset?

Record

As a group, record all the ways in which Pattie helped to change Noel's mindset.

_____

_____

_____

_____

_____

_____

_____

_____

_____

_____

_____

_____

_____

3 Learning from mistakes

We all make mistakes, but this is not a bad thing. Learning from your mistakes is one of the best ways to get better at something.

Babies learn to walk by trying and failing over and over again, until finally, they take their first steps.

To learn anything, you first need to try and fail. It will take time before you actually succeed.

Think about all your achievements to date. What steps did you take to get there?

Complete the timeline below to record the progress you have made since you were a baby.

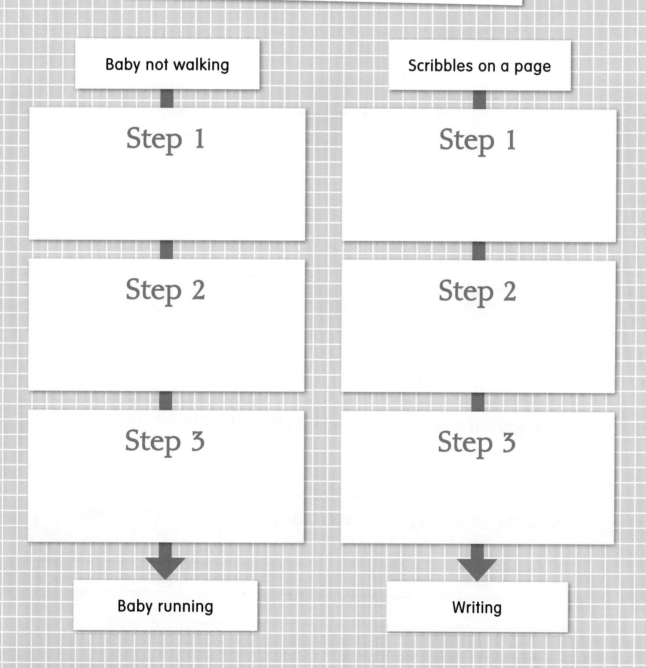

Baby not walking	Scribbles on a page
Step 1	Step 1
Step 2	Step 2
Step 3	Step 3
Baby running	Writing

23

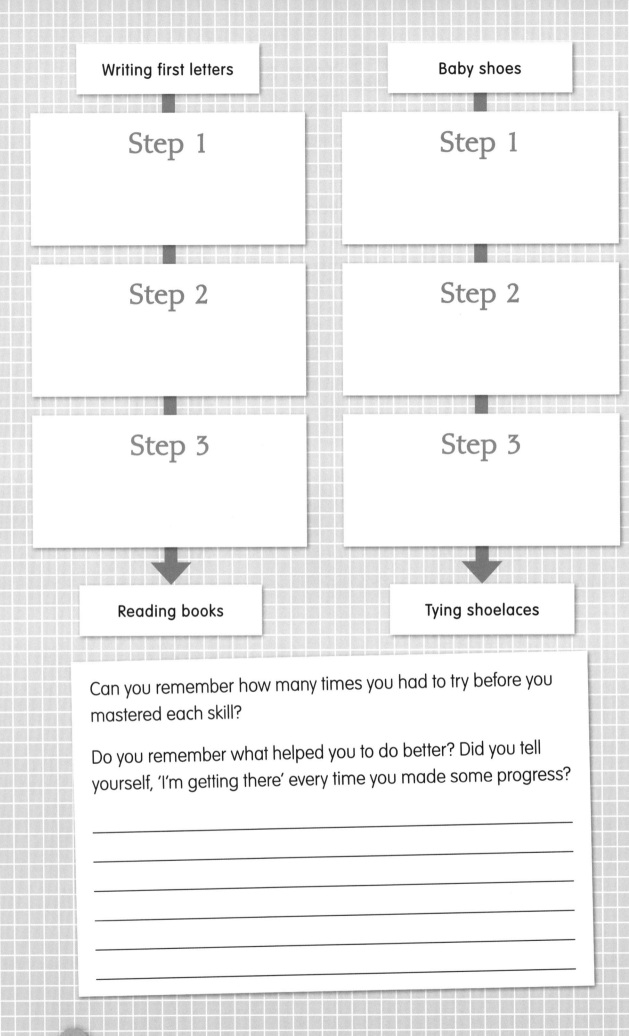

Writing first letters	Baby shoes
Step 1	Step 1
Step 2	Step 2
Step 3	Step 3
Reading books	Tying shoelaces

Can you remember how many times you had to try before you mastered each skill?

Do you remember what helped you to do better? Did you tell yourself, 'I'm getting there' every time you made some progress?

_____

_____

_____

_____

_____

_____

When you make a mistake, you may feel frustrated and disappointed. You can manage these situations by changing how you approach a challenge. Let's practise.

Consider the following examples. Choose a better way to manage each situation.

Question 1

Jack is upset. He cannot open his toy box by himself. He feels frustrated, so he kicks the box and hurts his toe.

Challenge	Open toy box
Current approach	Kicking box
Better approach	

Question 2

Matilda is trying to complete a maths exercise but she cannot understand the instructions. She says to herself, 'I can't do this. I am not smart enough.'

Challenge	Complete the maths exercise
Current approach	Say negative things
Better approach	

Question 3

Jermaine is trying to write a letter to his friend. He wants to post it before the post office closes. He is feeling rushed and starts crying. Then he yells, 'I give up!'

Challenge	Post the letter on time
Current approach	Give up and cry
Better approach	

If you are working towards something big, it can help to set smaller goals along the way. You can set goals in many ways. One very common way is called the SMART goals approach.

SMART stands for:

Specific

Measurable

Achievable

Realistic

Timely

Let's set a SMART goal.

Think about something you want to achieve. For instance, do you want to improve in a subject at school, score a goal in a soccer match or save your pocket money for something special?

Look at the example below. The goal is to get better at spelling.

Specific	I will get a better result in my spelling test this term than last term.
Measurable	I will get at least 7 out of 10 answers correct.
Achievable	Yes. I got 6 out of 10 last time and I can practise my spelling at home.
Realistic	Yes, definitely!
Timely	The test is in the last week of term.

Step 1

Set a goal for yourself.

_____

_____

_____

_____

_____

_____

_____

_____

_____

Step 2

Now break down your goal to fit into the SMART framework.

Specific	
Measurable	
Achievable	
Realistic	
Timely	

Step 3

Finally, plan some actions to help you achieve your goal.

Action	Things I need	Due date	Done?

A big part of achieving your goals is being organized and making sure you have time to work on them.

Look at the weekly calendar below. Choose one of your goals and find space in your week to work on it.

Step 1

Do you have any activities before or after school (for instance, soccer practice or music lessons)? Do you have any activities at the weekend? Do you have any hobbies you need to make time for?

Write these activities in the calendar.

Step 2

Now choose a goal and find a space during the week when you can work towards it. For example, if your goal is to get better at spelling, find time to practise.

	Monday	Tuesday	Wednesday	Thursday	Friday	Saturday	Sunday
Before school / Morning							
Lunch							
After school / Afternoon							
Evening							

5 Perseverance

Perseverance is when you keep working towards something, even when it is really difficult or it is taking longer than you expected.

It can be exhausting to push on when you are feeling tired of a task – but you can find the strength to keep going. Stay positive, set a clear goal and use positive self-talk to motivate yourself. Focus on each small achievable step in turn, like the flags in the desert scene below. With every forward movement you are making progress, even when that progress feels slow.

Read the scenario below. Use a word to fill each gap and complete the sentences.

laugh   determined   tried   carefully

proud   practise   better

Magda had to draw a picture of a tiger in the jungle for art. Magda did not love art, but she was _____ to try her best.

The first tiger she drew looked like an octopus! Somehow the legs were all wrong. Magda had a big _____ – this was going to be tricky. Then she turned over the paper and started again.

Magda's second attempt was _____ . She continued to _____ before she drew her final tiger on poster paper.

On the final tiger, she drew in the stripes slowly and _____ . Then she coloured them in. She glued big green leaves in the background for the jungle.

When she had finished, Magda was _____ that she had worked so hard. She was happy with her drawing – her tiger wasn't perfect but she had _____ her best.

My perseverance story

Can you think of a time when you kept trying to do something, like Magda with her tiger artwork?

This is called perseverance.

Write or draw about a time you:

Fixed a problem

Tried harder than ever

Did better than you expected

Didn't give up hope

► ACTIVITY ◄ Removing barriers

Sometimes, you will find it difficult to achieve your goals. However, you can overcome the barriers in your way:

- with perseverance
- by thinking creatively
- by asking for help.

In this activity, you will meet some children who are facing challenges. Can you choose some strategies to help them persevere?

Step 1

Turn to page 53. On this page, you will find a set of strategies. Remove the page and cut out the strategy cards.

Step 2

Look at the pictures and descriptions on pages 35–36.

Step 3

For each picture, choose a strategy that you think might help. Glue it in the box next to the picture. There are no right or wrong answers, just helpful ideas. You can choose more than one strategy for each picture if you like.

Zara has given up on her project because it seems too big.

Mateo keeps falling off his new skateboard. He is so angry he wants to give it away.

Emi tried out for the basketball A-team, but her coach has put her in the B-team instead.

Amir is doing some work on fractions, but he just cannot understand. He is frustrated.

Sofia has not yet made any friends at her new school. She is feeling discouraged.

6 Resilience

Resilience is different to perseverance.

- Perseverance is about pushing through, even when things are difficult.

- Resilience is about bouncing back from difficulties and challenges.

If you are resilient, you are able to cope with any setbacks that come your way. You can also adjust to changes in your life, such as:

- moving house

- missing out on something you expected

- getting a low score in a test

- losing a game of sport.

These things still hurt, but resilience means you can move on quickly, without feeling upset all day.

Most people have moments when they struggle to be resilient. Luckily, there are strategies you can use to help when you need a little extra resilience!

Let's find out more.

Let's measure our resilience.

Take this resilience quiz and see how you cope when things do not go as planned. How quickly do you recover from disappointment?

Question 1

It is your birthday. As a special treat, Dad is taking you and a friend to see a movie. On the way, the car breaks down. You miss the start of the movie while you wait for the tow truck to arrive.

What do you do?

A Get upset. Yell and scream at Dad and the tow truck driver for ruining your birthday.

B Feel disappointed and make some angry faces, but try not to be too upset with Dad. It is not his fault the car broke down.

C Feel sad but remember it could have been worse. At least your friend is there to make the situation more fun!

Question 2

You make a beautiful poster for the class poster competition. But while you are on the bus to school, a stranger spills coffee all over your poster! It is ruined.

What do you do?

A Yell at the stranger and cry. Order the bus driver to turn the bus around so you can go home and start working on a new poster!

B Feel annoyed but try to mop up the coffee with some tissues. You will just have to hand in the poster with coffee stains.

C Start planning how you can prepare another poster before the competition. If you rush into school and ask your teacher, you may have time to make a new one.

Question 3

At playtime, you get separated from your friends and cannot find them anywhere. You are all alone in the busy playground.

What do you do?

A Sit in a quiet corner and cry, hoping the bell will ring soon.

B Walk around the playground looking for your friends until the bell goes.

C Join a game with some other children.

Question 4

It is school photo day and everyone has remembered to wear their full navy-blue school uniform – except you! You are going to be the only child in the school photograph wearing a green tracksuit and trainers.

What do you do?

A Hide in the toilets until the photograph has been taken, and hope nobody notices.

B Call your parents from the school office and ask them to drop off your blue uniform!

C Go to the school office and ask if there are any spare uniforms. Someone will be able to help you.

Question 5

You are invited to a birthday sleepover with your best friends. But when you get there, everyone thinks it is funny to ignore you.

What do you do?

A Call your Dad and ask him to come and collect you straight away.

B Go and find your friend's little brother and play with him instead.

C Tell them it is not funny and speak to their parents. This has to stop.

The cope-ometer

Look back at your answers. How many As did you choose? How many Bs? How many Cs?

Now look at the table below to find out how you cope with setbacks.

Mostly As	Mostly Bs	Mostly Cs
You are still learning to be resilient. When you find yourself in a difficult situation, try to take a deep breath and find a way forward.	You are still practising problem solving – good job! It can be difficult to find solutions and you will continue to get better with practice.	You are very resilient! When something goes wrong, you get right back up and keep trying. Well done.

▶ REFLECTION ◀

Can you think about a time when you showed resilience?
Remember, asking for help is a way of coping.

Answer the questions below, by writing or drawing pictures
about times when you were resilient.

1   I showed resilience by asking for help …

2   I showed resilience by learning more about …

3   I showed resilience by improving …

4   I showed resilience by …

Being resilient is also about your attitude, and how you think about setbacks. If you know you have people to help you, and you know you have all the skills you need to be resilient, you will be more confident.

Think about these questions. Write 'Yes' or 'No' in each of the boxes below.

Do you know a supportive adult?	
Do you have some helpful friends?	
Can you laugh and be creative to help you solve problems?	
Do you have a growth mindset?	
Could you use a website or other tools to help you bounce back?	

Describe a time when …

1 Someone helped you to overcome a challenge.

2 A friend supported you when you needed their help.

3 You used your humour and creativity to solve a problem.

4 You used positive words and attitudes to bounce back.

5 You were able to find ideas online or in your community to solve a problem.

We all experience changes in life, such as the arrival of a new baby or when a friend moves away. Some changes are good, but others will take time to get used to.

Read the stories below and write down some ideas to help the children cope with change. The first example has been done to help you get started. Think of as many ideas as you can to help make the situation better.

Mrs Herring is leaving the school.
The children are very upset.

They could ask for her email address so they can stay in touch.

They could write letters or make cards to tell her how much they care.

What are your ideas to make this situation better?

Serina has been put in a class without any of her friends.

Gus is really worried about moving up to the part of the school where the older, bigger children are.

Raj's mum is going to work overseas for three months and he will not be able to see her.

Atiya's mum and dad are adopting a new baby. Atiya is worried they will not have time for her anymore.

Step 1

Do you have any changes coming up?

Make a list of new things that will happen for you in the future.

_____

_____

_____

_____

_____

_____

It is helpful to start thinking about changes before they happen. This will help you to prepare. You cannot be ready for everything, but there are usually things you can do to learn more about a new situation.

For example, if you were starting at a new school, you could try these things to help you feel more prepared.

- Go and explore the playground.

- Look at the school website.

- Ask them to send you a yearbook or a photo of your new class.

- Phone the school to ask for more information.

Step 2

Think about the changes you wrote down in Step 1.

For each change, write or draw ideas about how you can prepare.

Change	How to prepare

▶ REFLECTION ◀

You have come to the end of this book. What have you learned?
What ideas and strategies will you implement?

Glossary

Fixed mindset

If you have a fixed mindset, you feel as though you cannot get better at things, even if you practise. You are unwilling to try new things because you are worried you might fail.

Growth mindset

If you have a growth mindset, you believe you can get better at things if you try. You are willing to try new things, even if they are not easy.

Mindset

The way we think about problems and challenges and the way we try to solve them.

Motivation

The feeling or impulse that encourages you to do something.

Negative self-talk

When we think about something in a negative way (for example, saying, 'I can't do this') and it changes how we feel about it.

Perseverance

When we keep working towards something, even if it is difficult or it is taking longer than expected.

Positive reinforcement

When someone else uses positive words such as, 'You can do this!'

Positive self-talk

When we use positive words such as, 'I can do this!'

Resilience

Being able to bounce back from difficulties and challenges.

Self-motivation

When we do things because we want to.

Setbacks

Temporary problems – things that hold you up or make things difficult.

Strategy

A practical solution.

Templates

Word cards for Activity on pages 18–19

Cut out the following words. ✂

exciting	challenge	face	yet

still improving	will	motivated

satisfying	still learning	growth	easier

Templates

▶ ACTIVITY ◀ Removing barriers

Strategy cards for Activity on pages 34–36

Cut out the following sentences. ✂

Try setting mini-goals	Break down the task into smaller tasks	Find someone to practise with
Ask a parent for ideas on how to get started	Use a timer and take short breaks	Ask for feedback from an expert
Ask a grown-up to explain it in a different way	Set a timetable for your practice and try to create good habits	Use positive words to think about the problem in another way
Talk to someone else who has had this challenge and ask what they did	Focus on getting started and doing your best; don't aim for perfection	Take a break, practise some mindful breathing or do something else you enjoy; then try again with a clearer mind